Marley Freeman

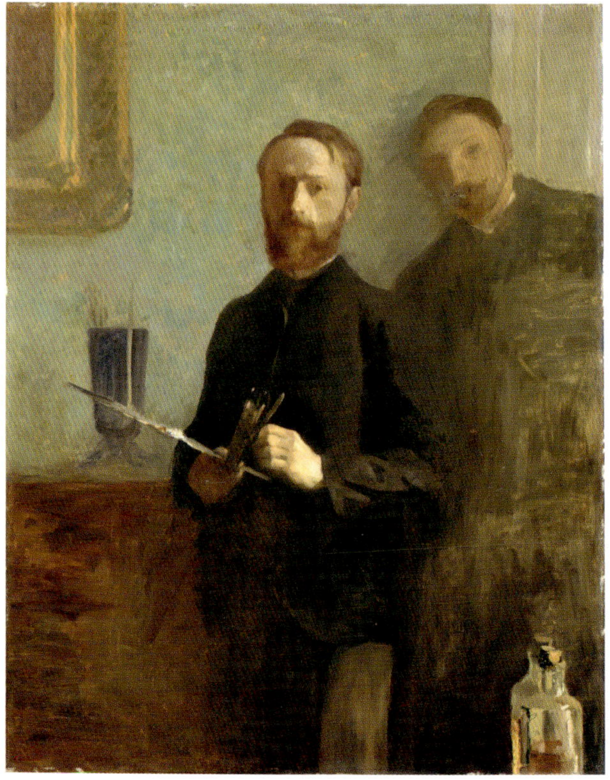

Edouard Vuillard, *Self-Portrait with Waroquy* (1889), oil on canvas,
36½ × 28½ inches. Gift of Alex M. Lewyt, 1955 (55.173).
The Metropolitan Museum of Art, New York, NY, USA.
Photo Credit: Image copyright © The Metropolitan Museum of Art.
Image source: Art Resource, NY

Vuillard was only twenty-three when he painted this uncanny work, and he can be identified as the figure on the left, with a palette and paintbrushes in hand. Behind him is his friend, Waroquy, a cigarette between his lips. Waroquy's ghostlike body appears unfinished, his face less defined, washed-out. A small, rounded bottle is placed to the lower right of the canvas; it is also doubled, and flattened. It then becomes clear that this is a mirror image, a depiction of a reflection. According to one of Vulliard's journal entries, he posed in front a mirror in his grandmother's bedroom to produce the painting.[5] The work is indicative of Vuillard's move away from mimetically capturing nature and toward a more fluctuating, imprecise field of vision—between sensation and imagination—which would go on to become the lifeblood of his practice, and a major (if undervalued) crossroads in the history of art.

Another inspiration cited by Marley: Maine. Many of the works in *Park Closes at Midnight* are based on memories of the state's cold, crystal clear saltwater, and its rocky seashores bordered by pine trees and shrubs.[6] For me, the paintings summon nostalgia for swimming in Lincolnville—at a beach where the Ducktrap River flows into Penobscot Bay—and it was a pleasure to have the opportunity to be there while thinking through much of this essay. While in Maine, I caught a wonderful, if too small, show at Rockland's Farnsworth Art Museum: *Slab City Rendezvous*. The exhibition took its title from a 1964 painting by Red Grooms, which depicts a party scene on Slab City Road in Lincolnville. The show brought together a group of New York–based artists who had been summering in Maine since in the 1950s and '60s, and the works on view, nearly all figurative and sometimes realist paintings, wrestled with the dominant style of their day: abstract expressionism. Among works by Alex Katz, Rackstraw Downes, and Mimi Gross, a painting by Lois Dodd caught my eye, because it was one of the only works to retain a sense of abstraction.

Dodd's *Clam Diggers* (1958–59), a jumble of shapes in muted browns, grays, and blues, at first appears entirely abstract. But on closer inspection, a figure emerges in the center of the painting: a hunched-over person tunneling into the ground, silhouetted by the sea. The composition reminded me of Marley's work, particularly that aforementioned figure in *Erasure Alert*, but also *Nikki* (2018) and *For the Night* (2018), where shapes of unmodulated color create a bold patterning and almost seem to turn in and churn, wavelike, into one another. Those paintings aren't quite seascapes—they are nonrepresentational—but they find easy kinship with Dodd's work.

Decked Out, 2018–19
Oil on linen
14½ × 12⅝ inches

14

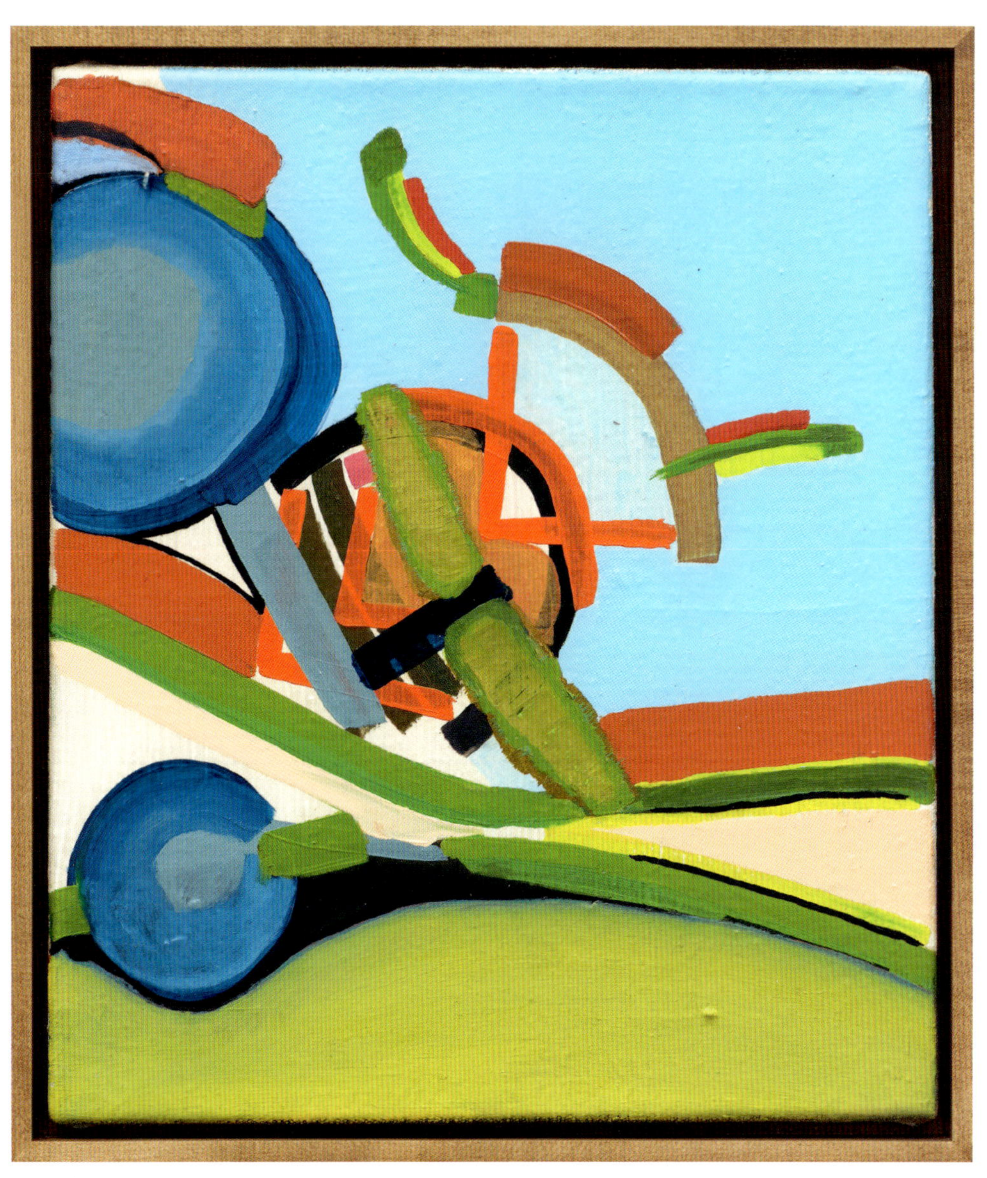

Vinyl Sunburn, 2016
Acrylic on canvas
19½ × 20¾ inches

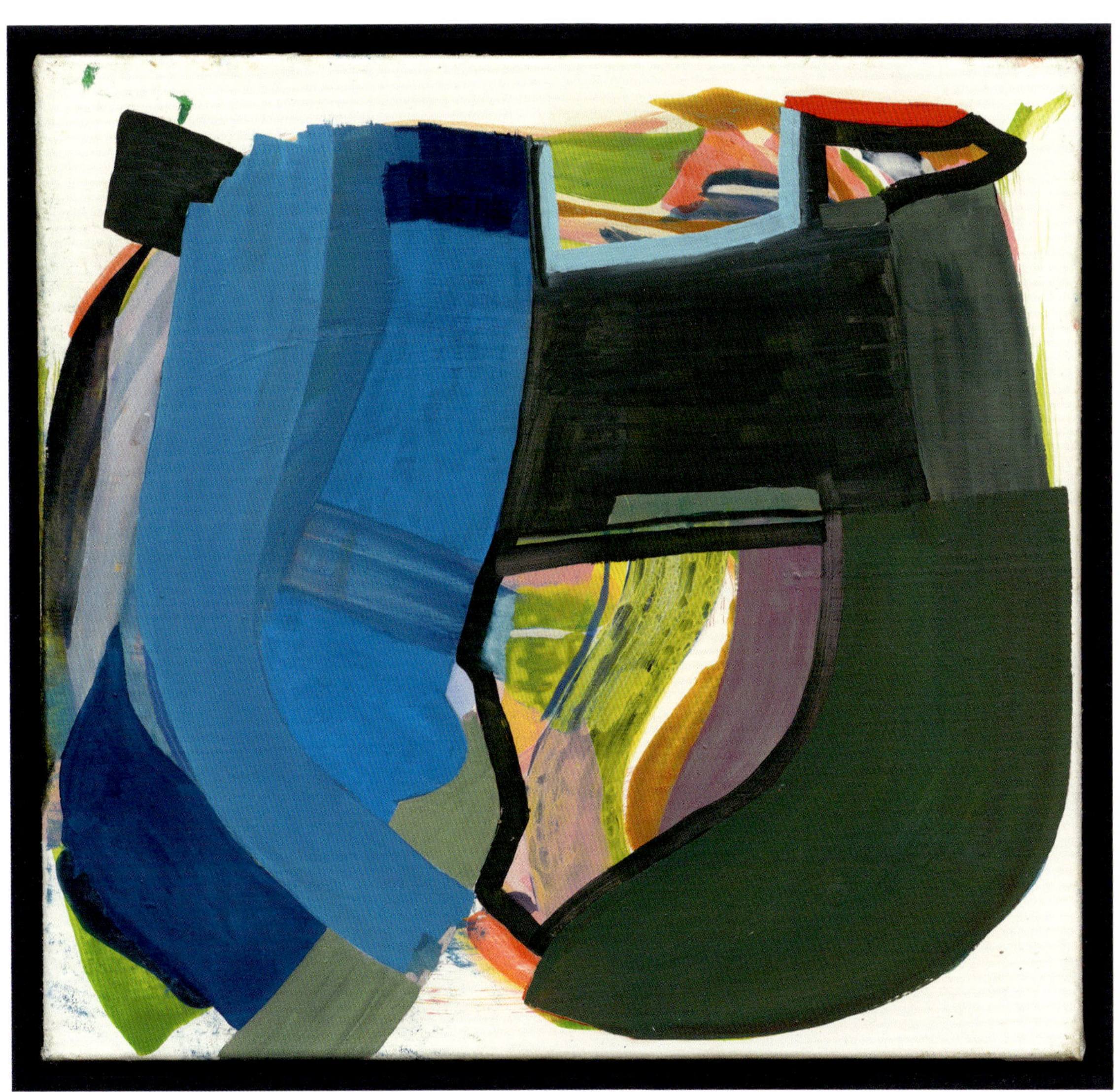

Crimes-Crepes, 2019
Oil on linen
18⅝ × 14⅝ inches

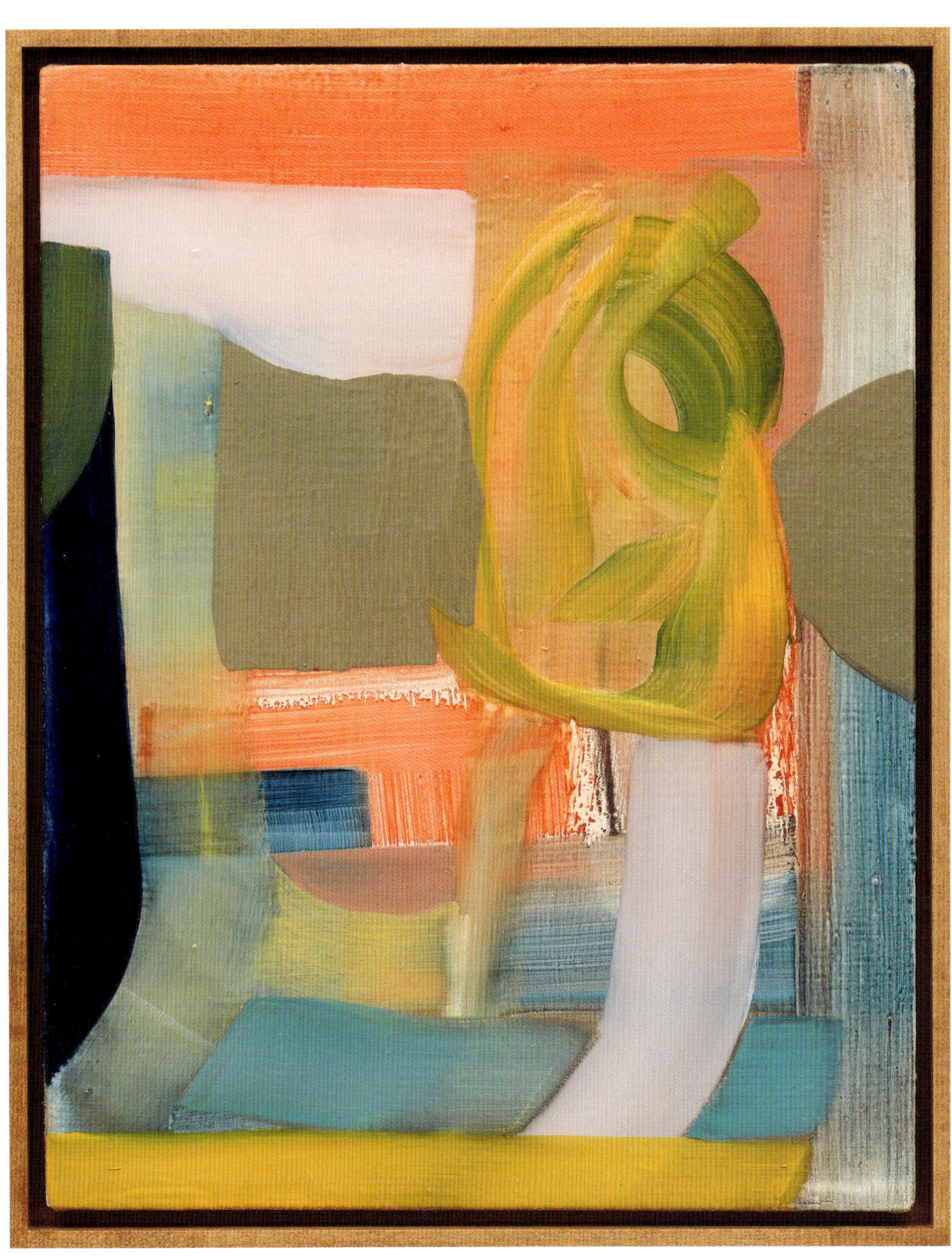

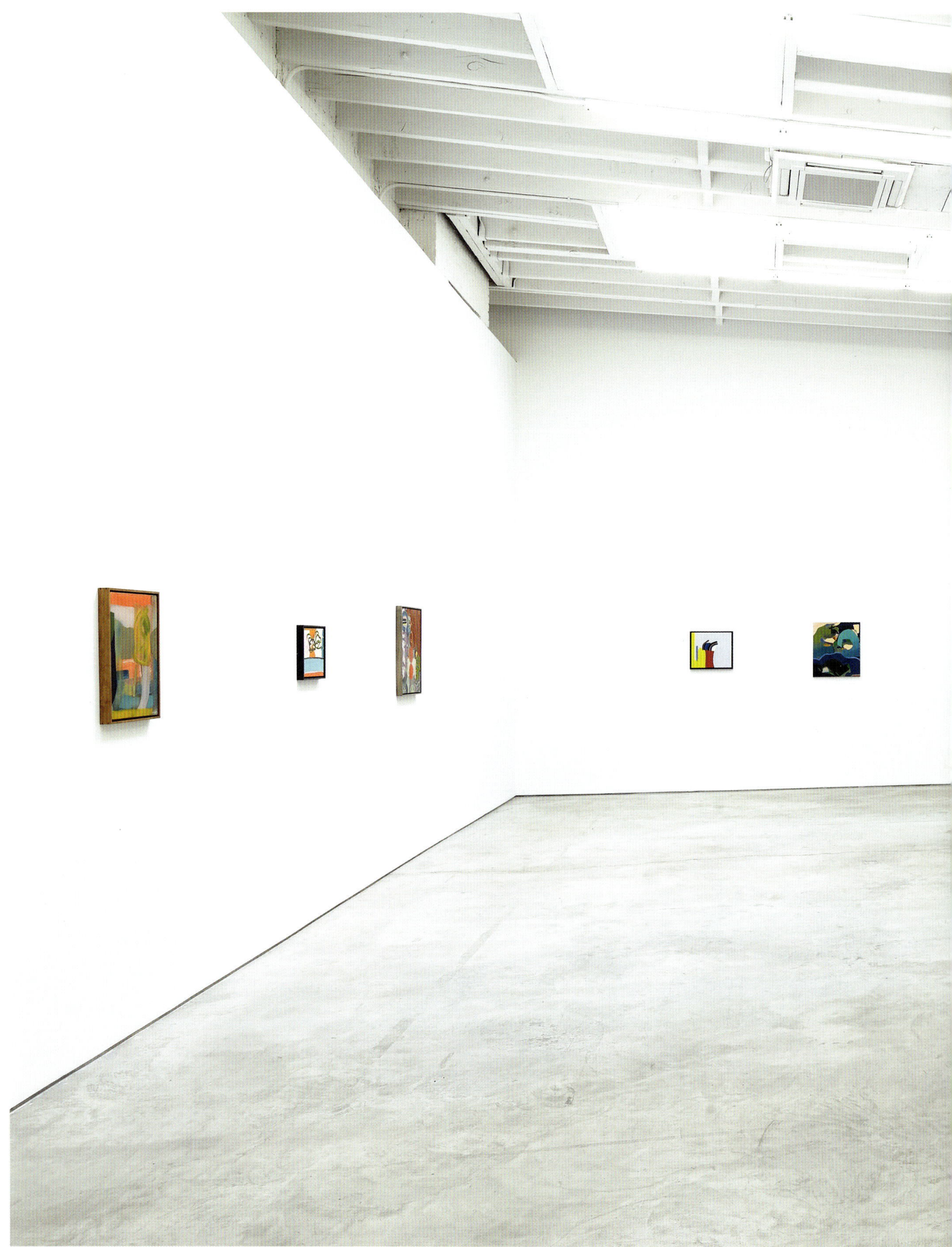

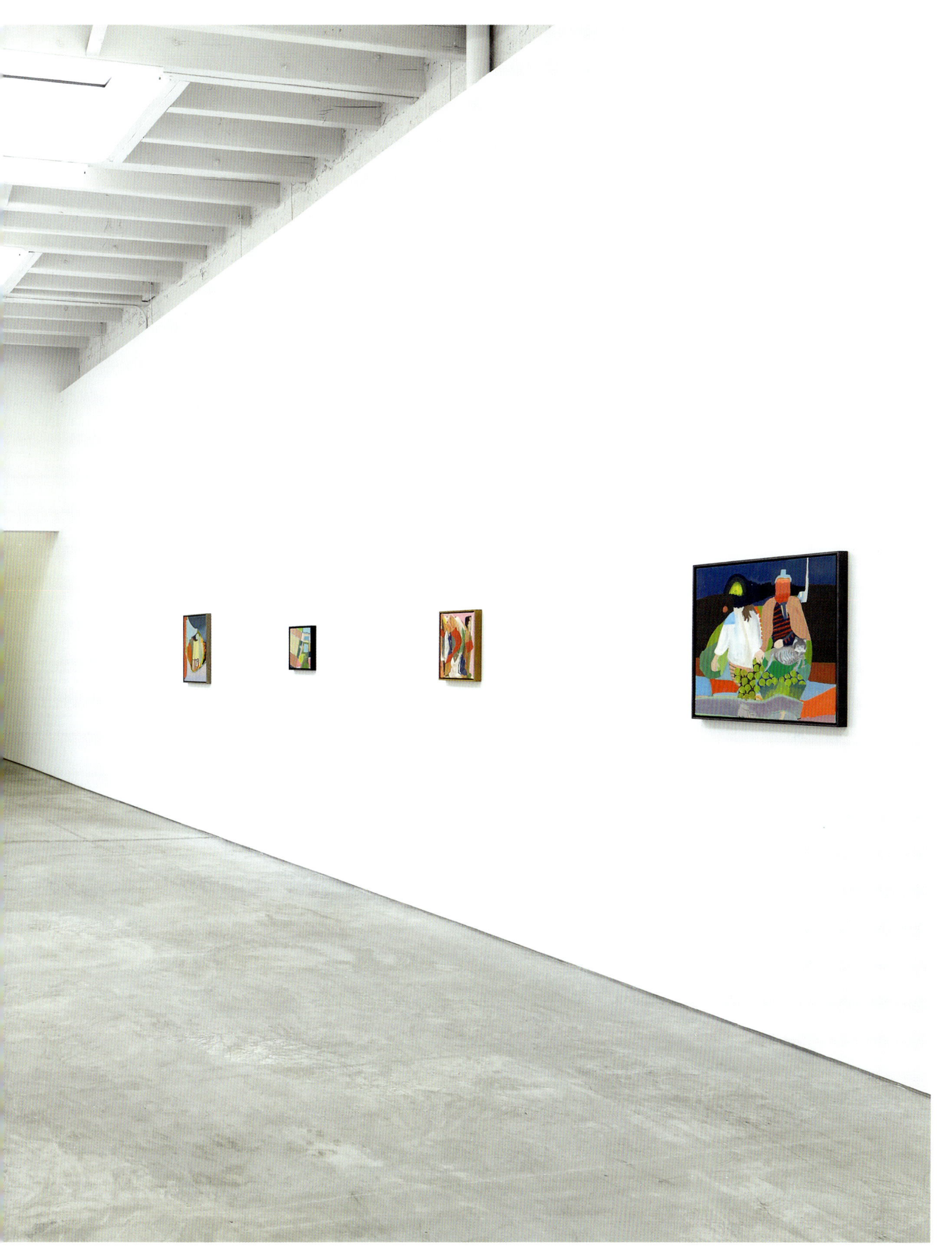

Humaneness, 2018
Oil on linen
10½ × 12⅝ inches

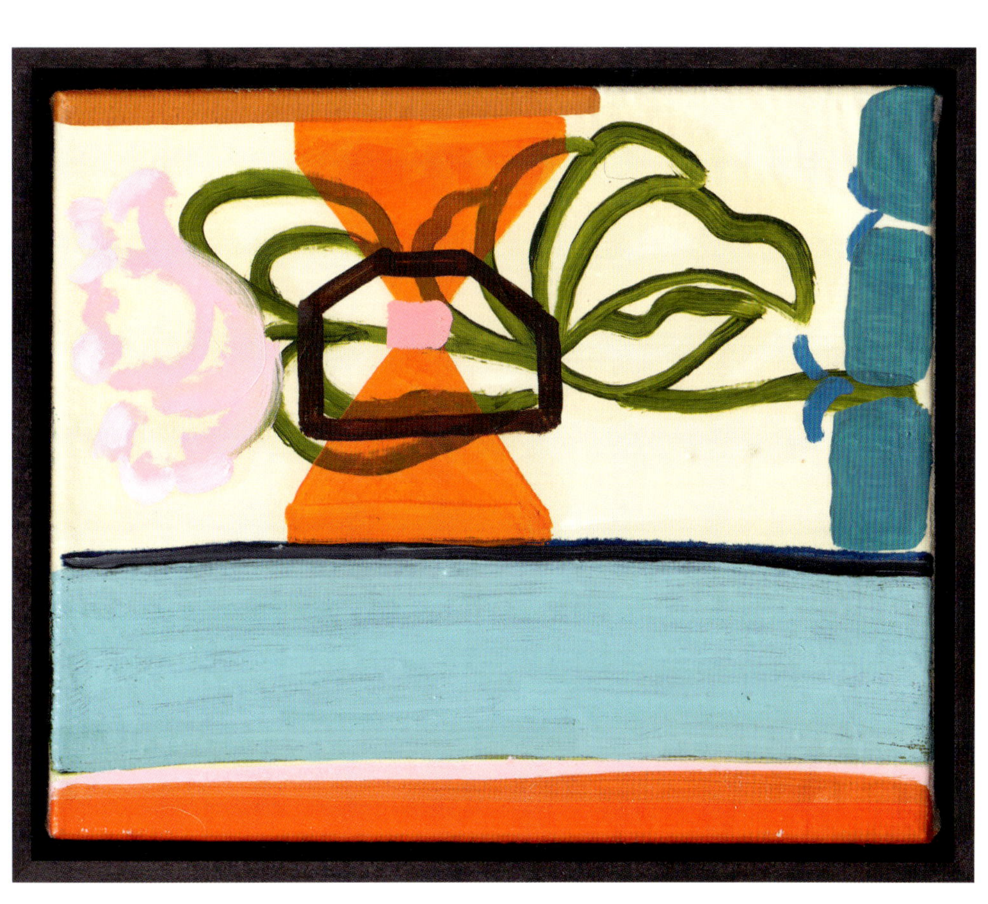

The Rear View, 2018
Oil on canvas
22⅝ × 18½ inches

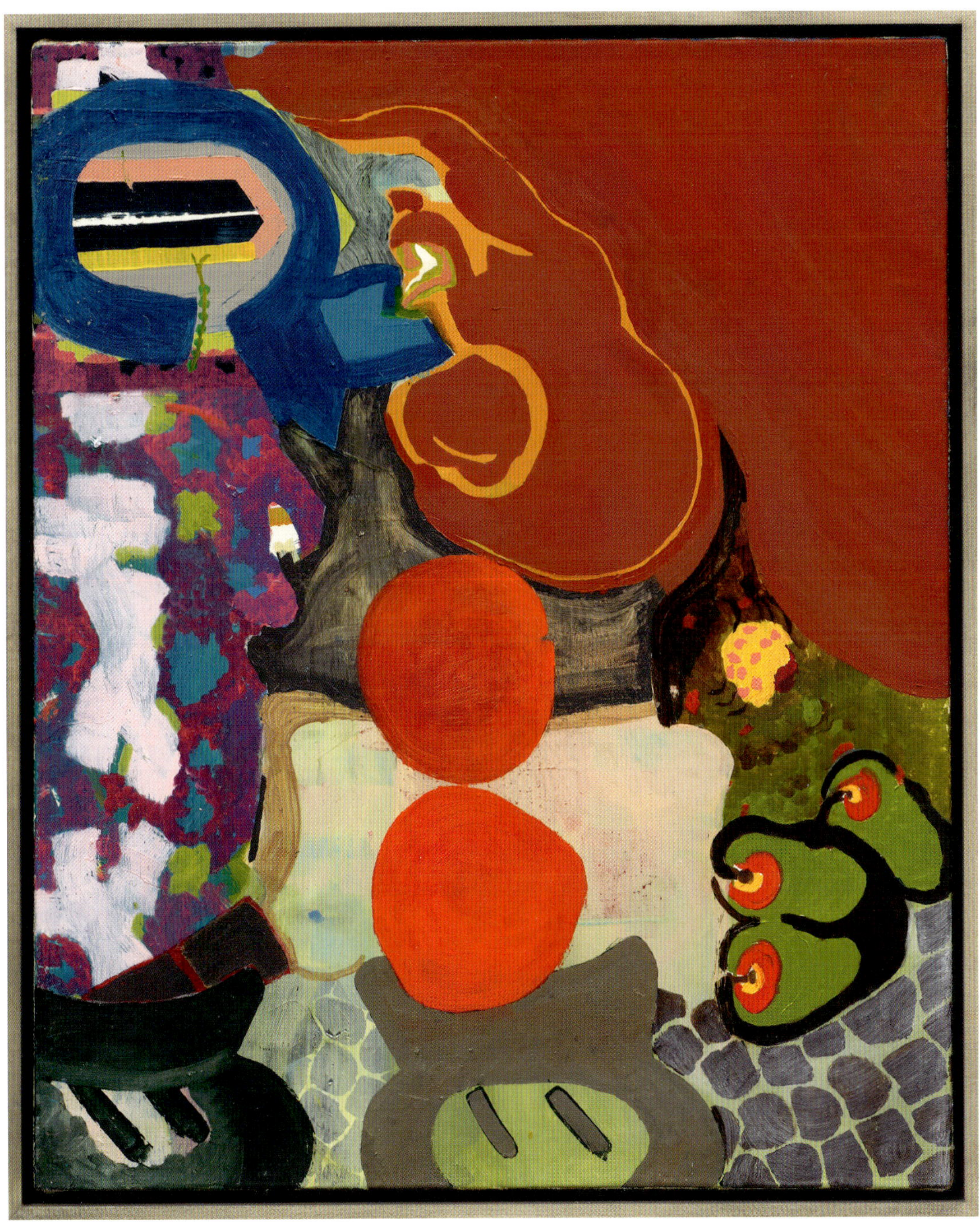

Naked Taste, 2019
Oil on linen
14½ × 16⅝ inches

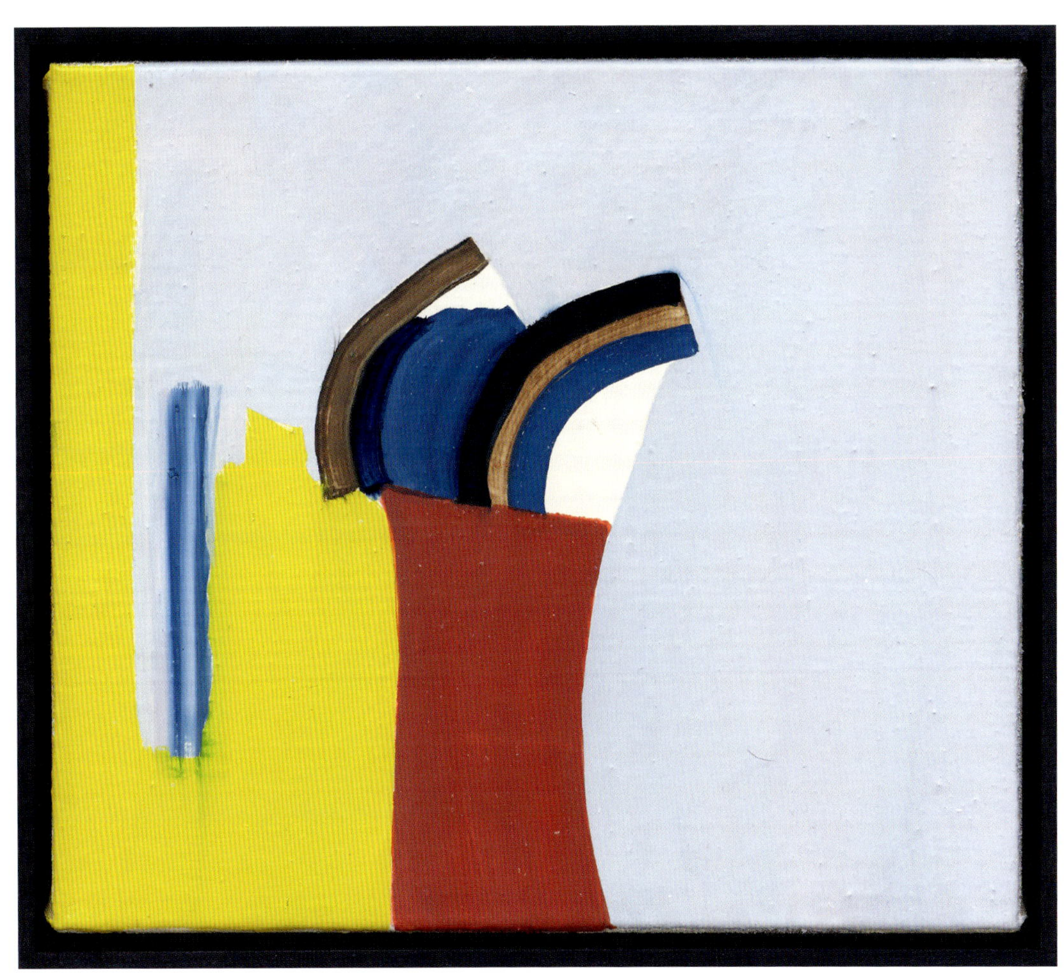

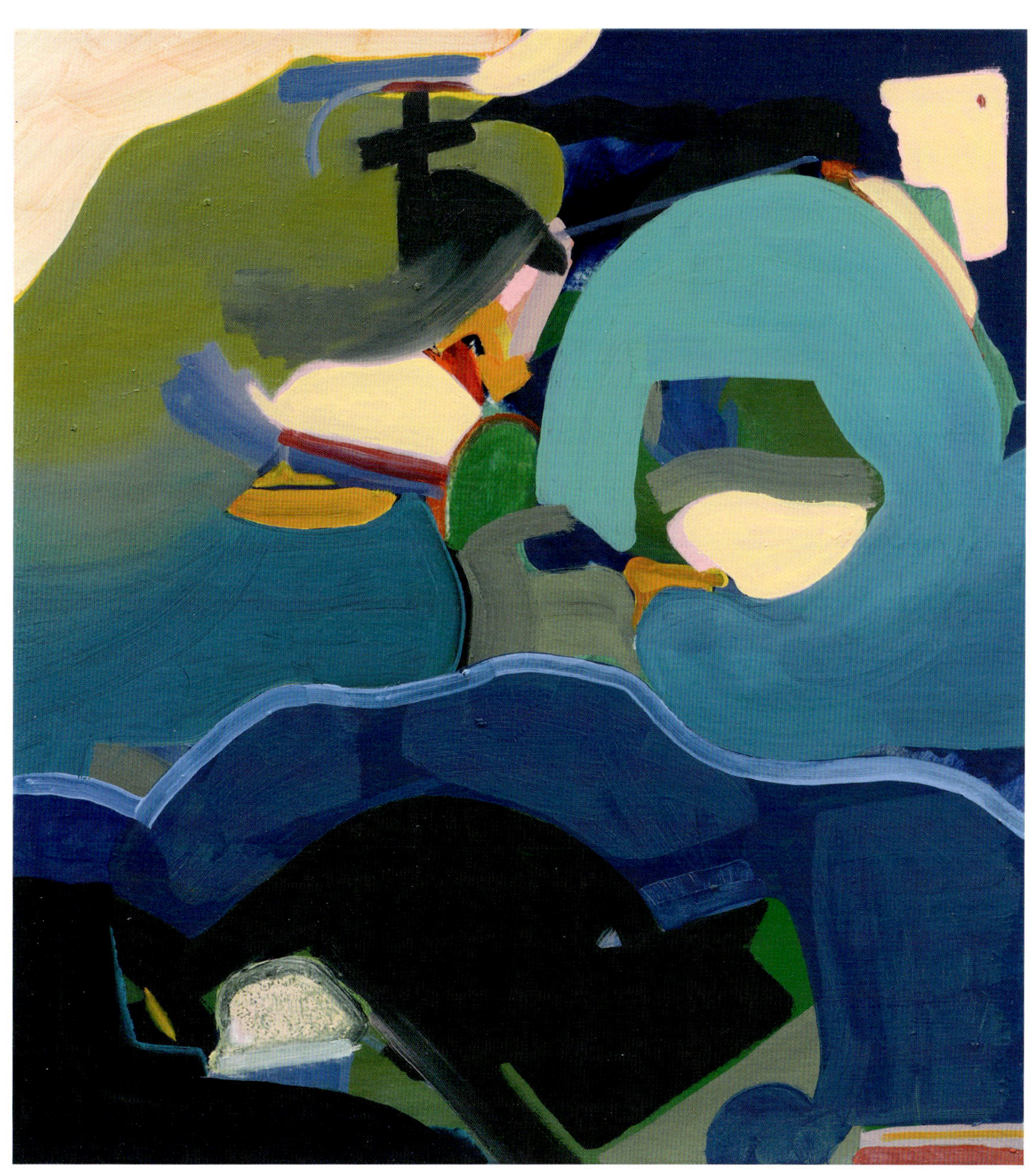

Nikki, 2018
Oil on linen
20⅝ × 18⅝ inches

30

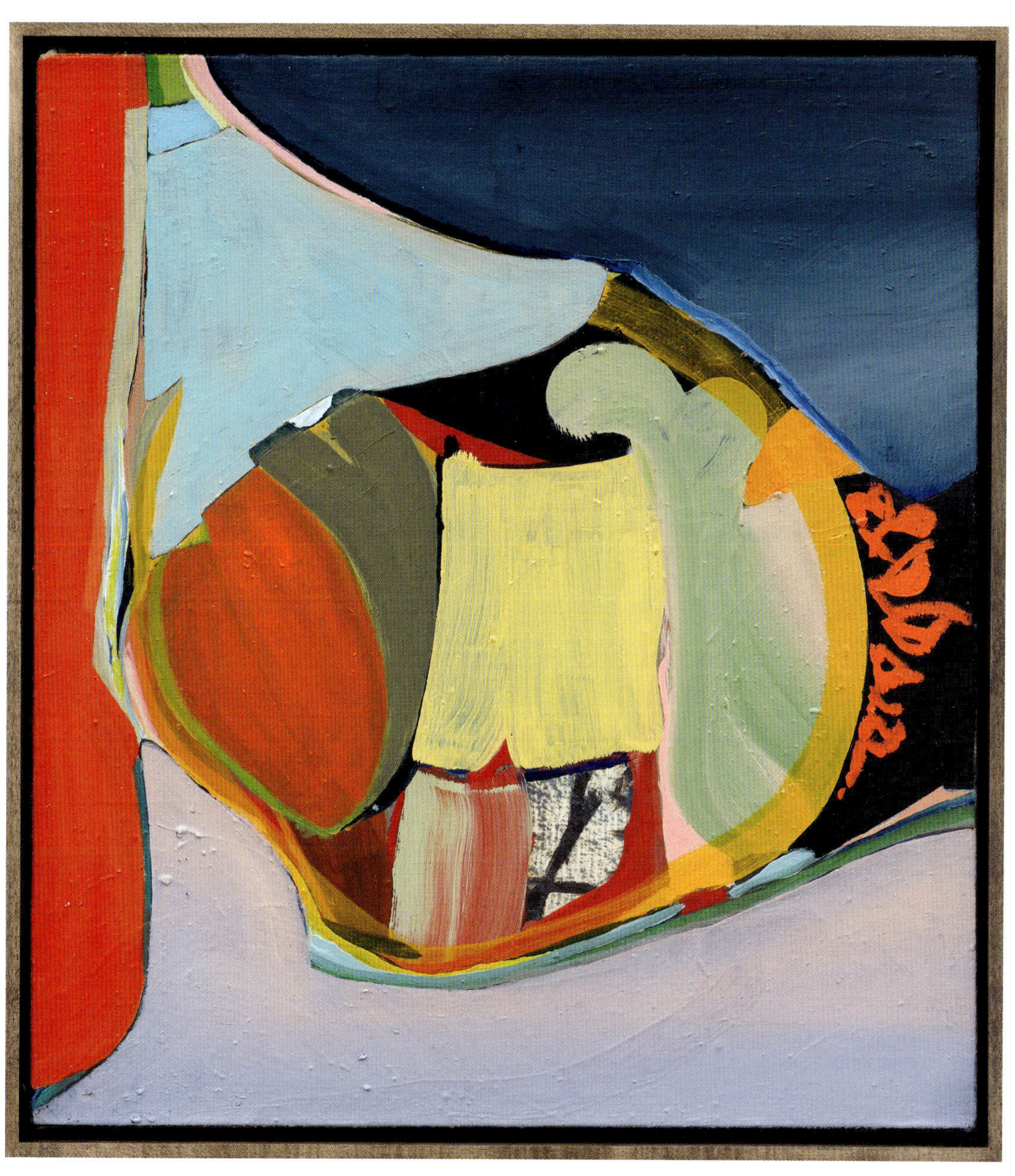

Fleeced Paint, 2019
Oil on linen
10⅝ × 11⅝ inches

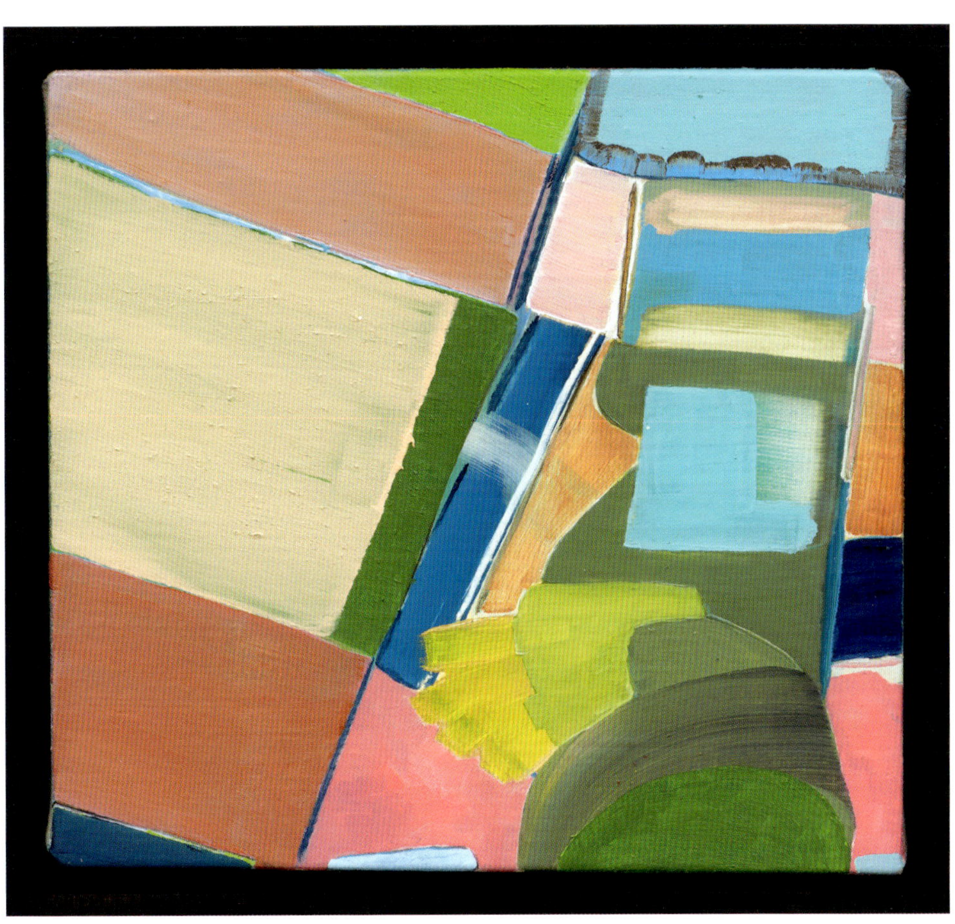

Tall Grass, 2016
Acrylic on canvas
13⅝ × 11⅝ inches

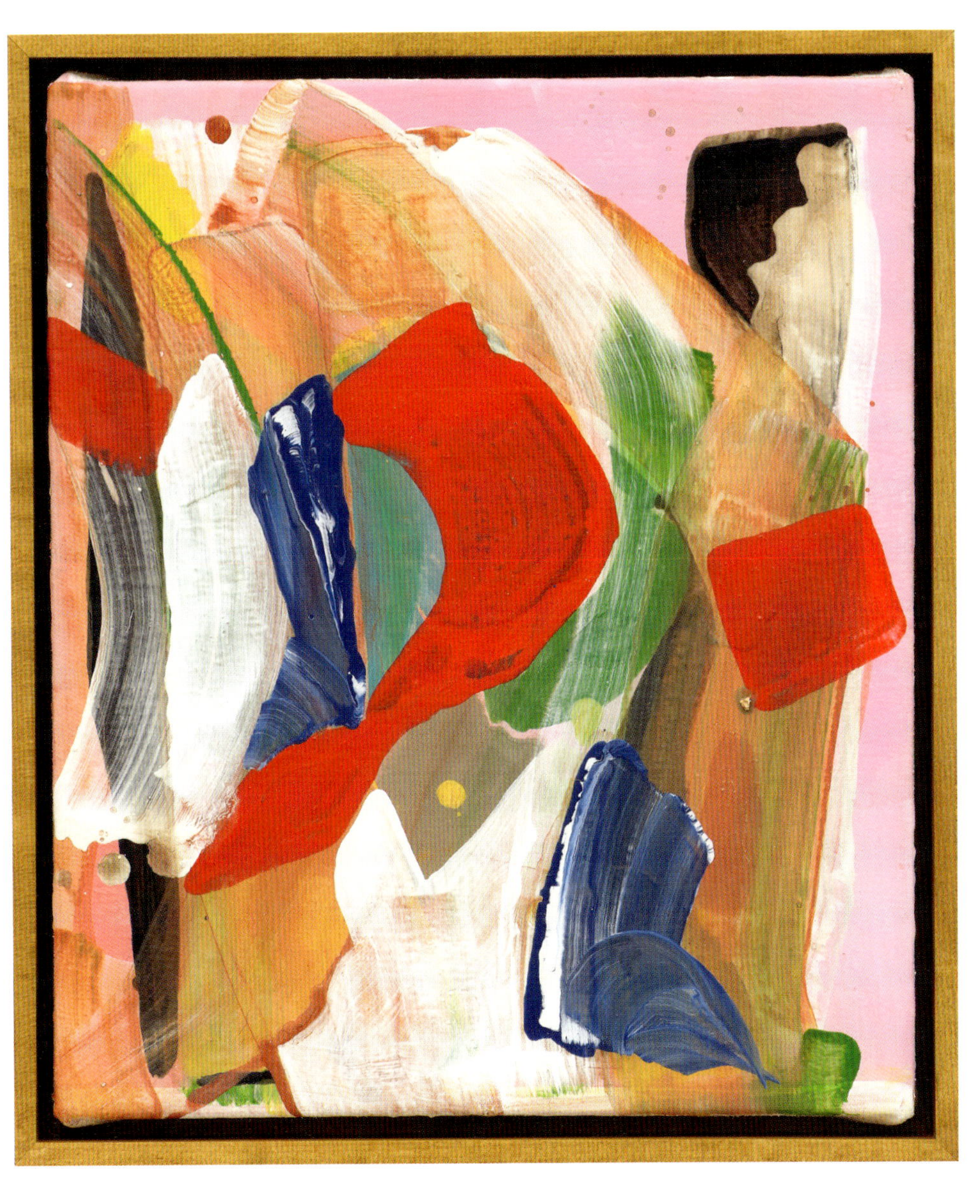

Ampersand, 2018
Oil on canvas
22⅝ × 24½ inches

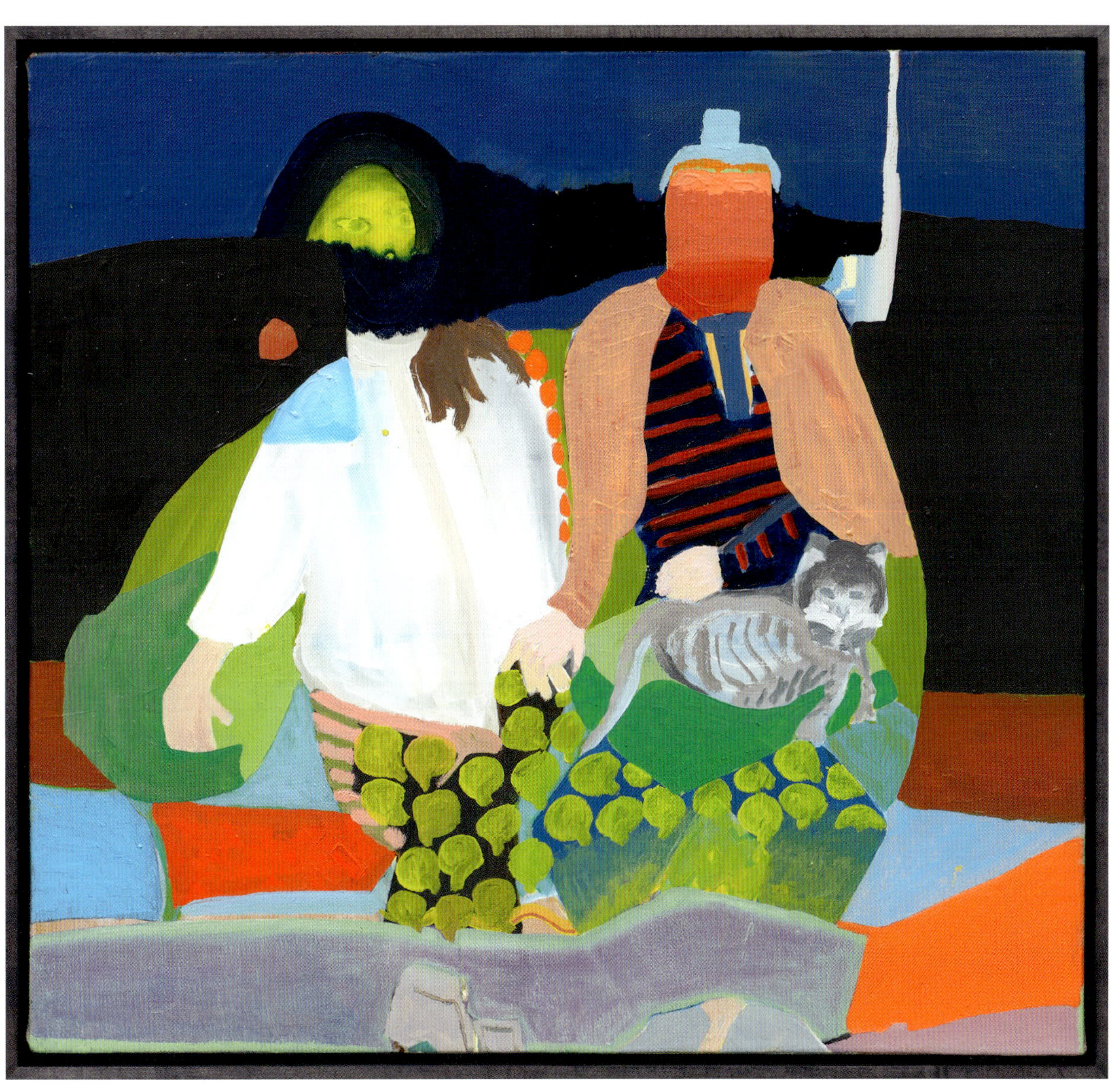

Old Stone, 2017–19
Oil and acrylic on canvas
8½ × 10⅝ inches

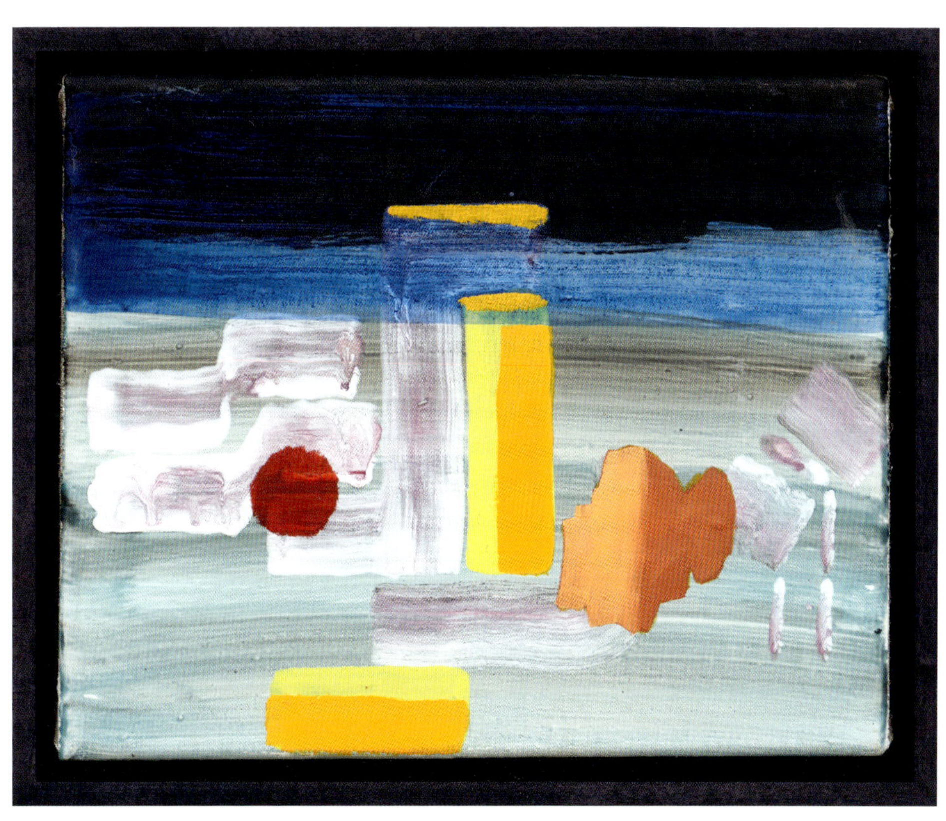

Ha Ir Re, 2019
Oil on linen
10½ × 9½ inches

40

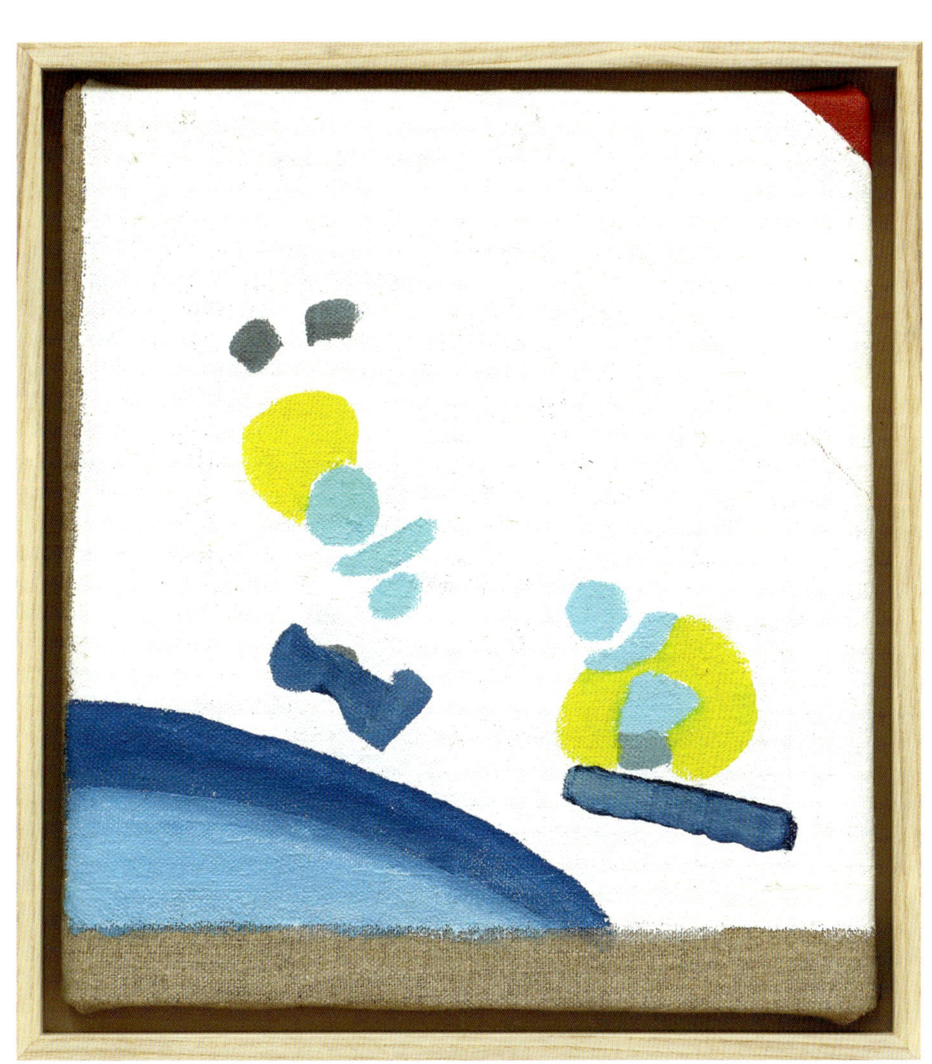

See Past, 2019
Oil on linen
20 5/8 × 18 5/8 inches

42

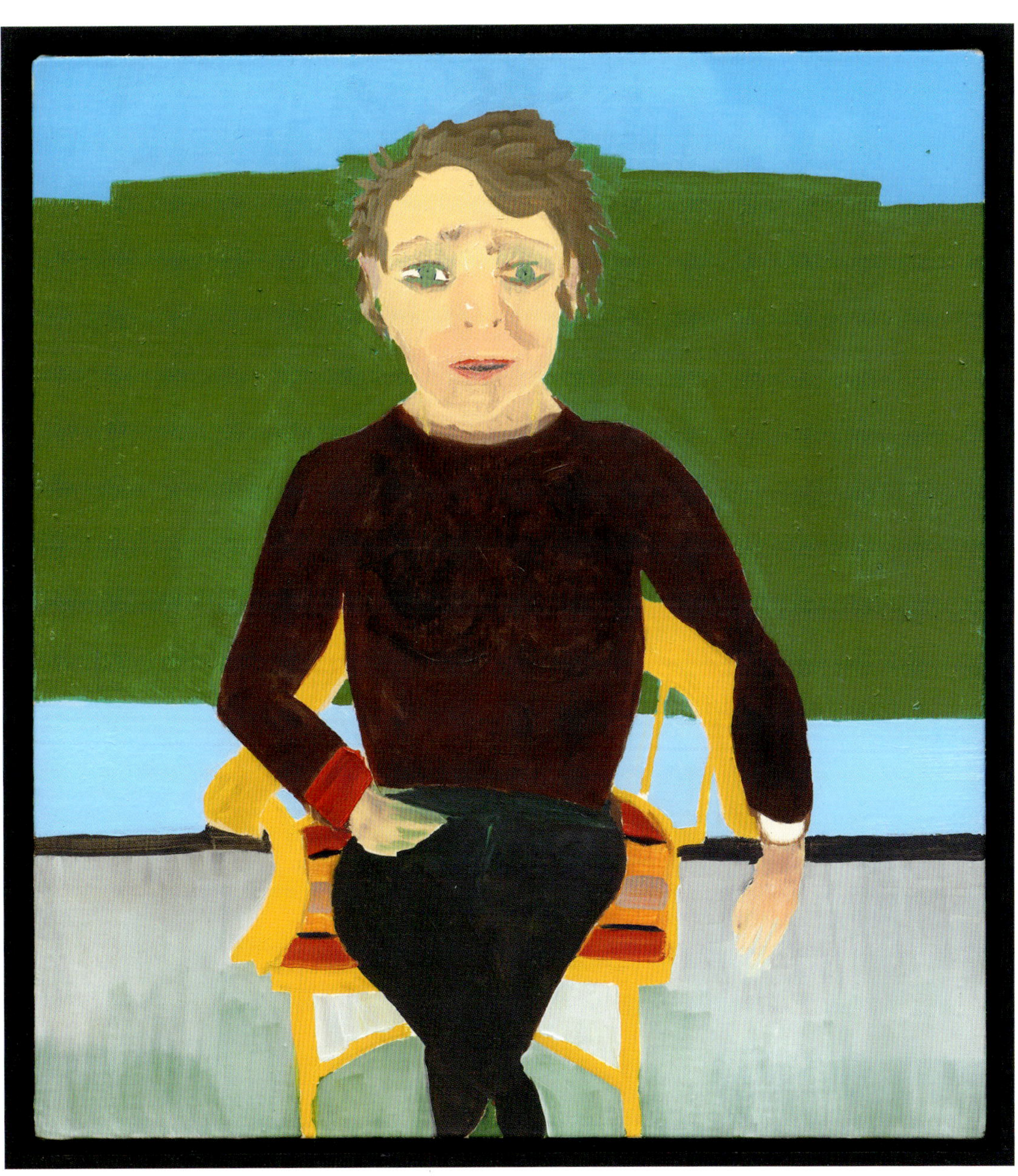

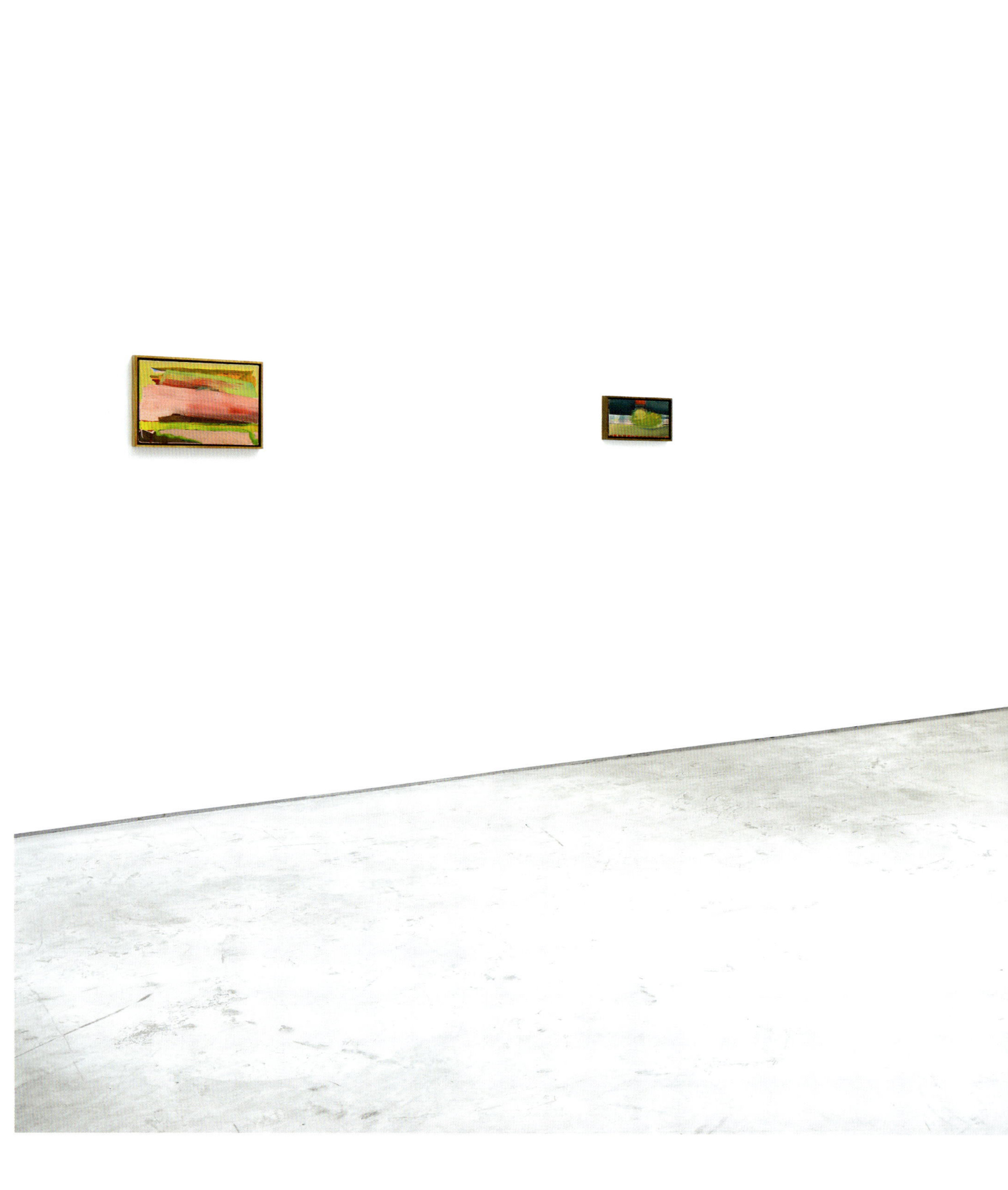

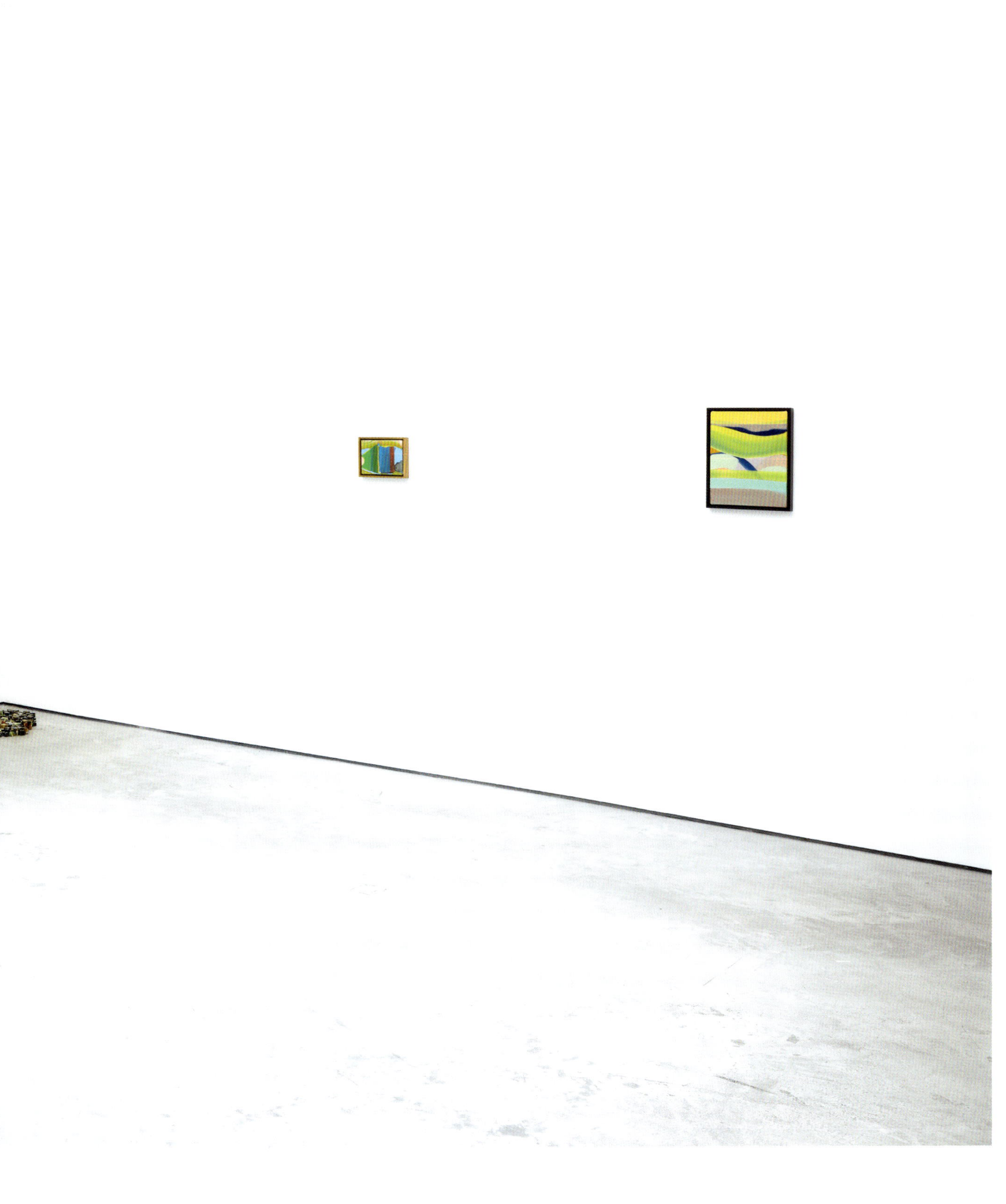

Face to Earth, 2017
Oil and acrylic on linen
10¾ × 12¾ inches

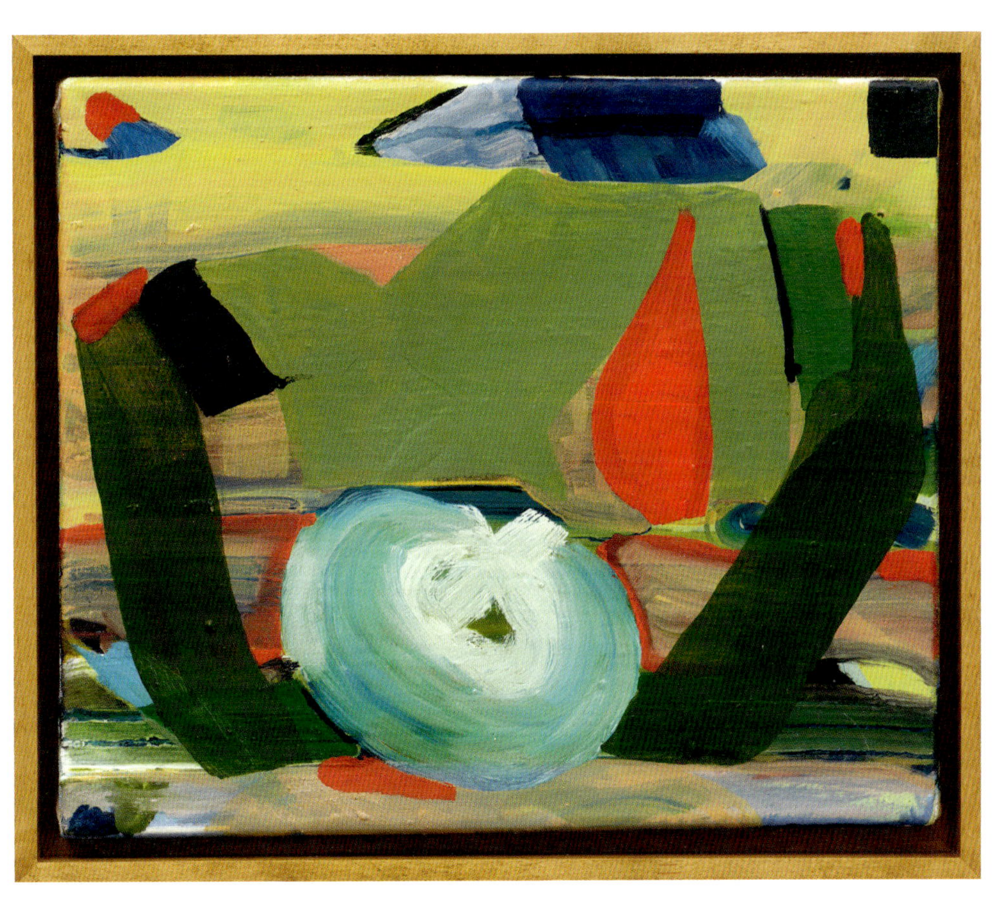

Sagacious Hose in the Alley, 2019
Oil on linen
14⅝ × 11⅝ inches

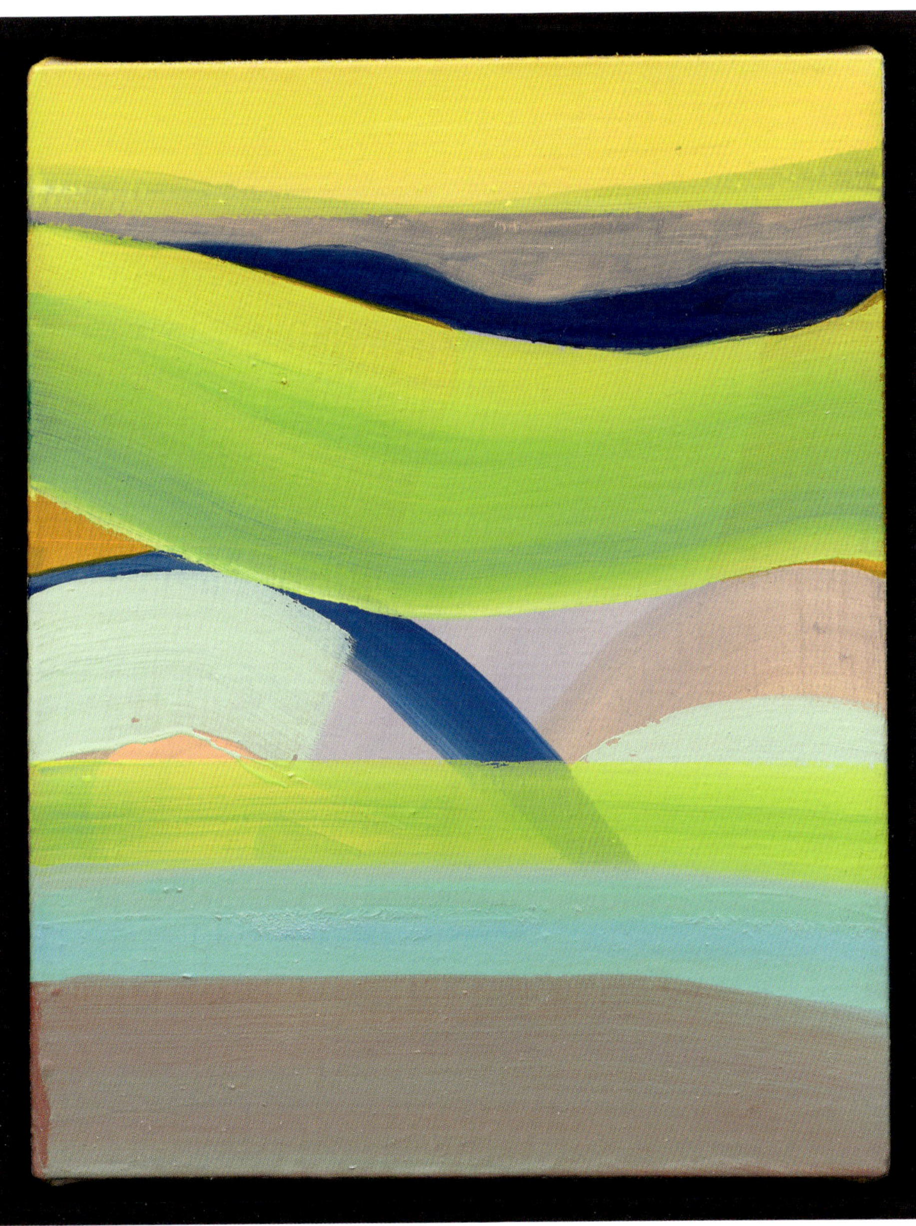

Navel to Ear, 2019
Oil on linen
6½ × 8⅝ inches

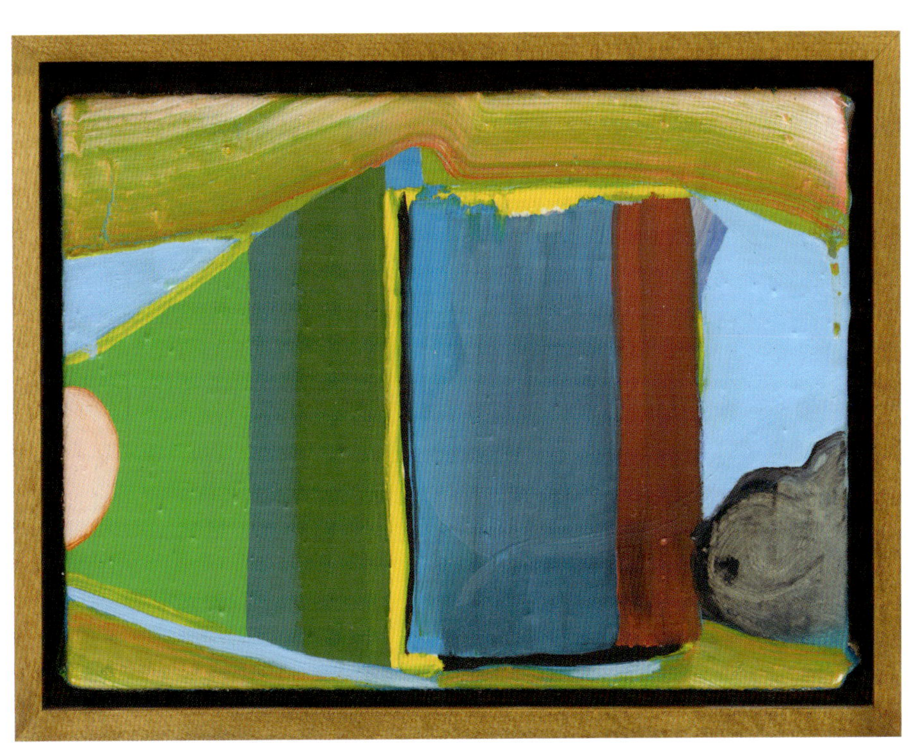

Hairs of the Hole, 2019
Oil on linen
6⅝ × 11⅝ inches

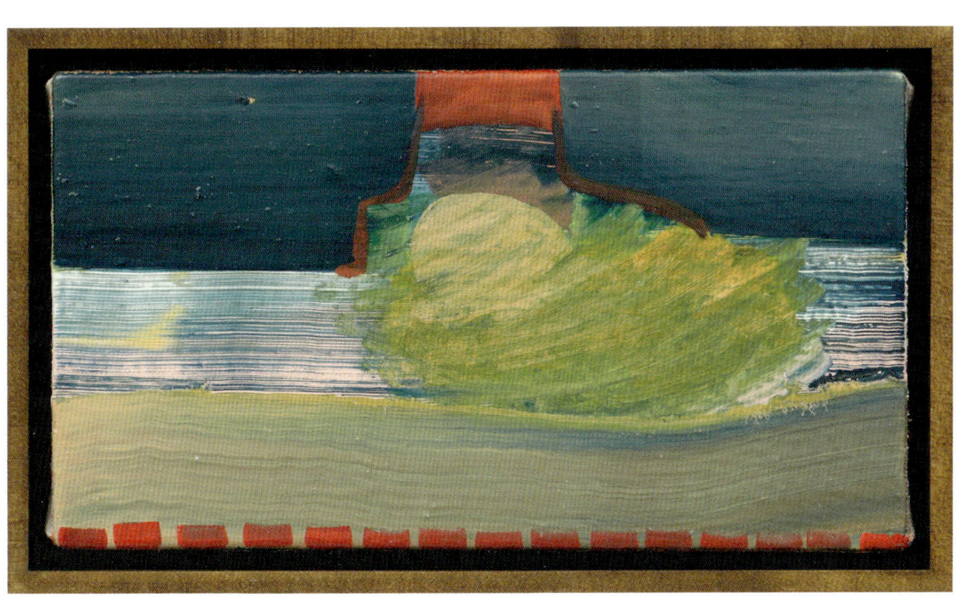

Bath, 2016–19
Acrylic on canvas
11½ × 15¾ inches

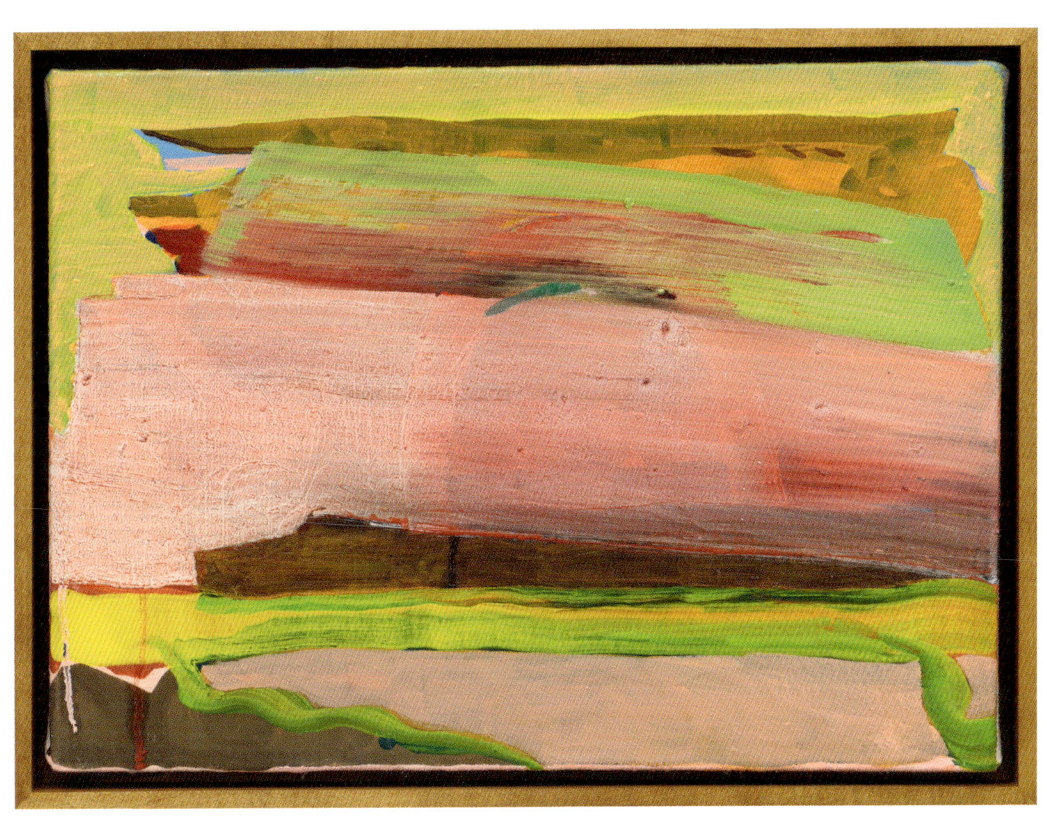

Erasure Alert, 2019
Acrylic on canvas
8½ × 10⅝ inches

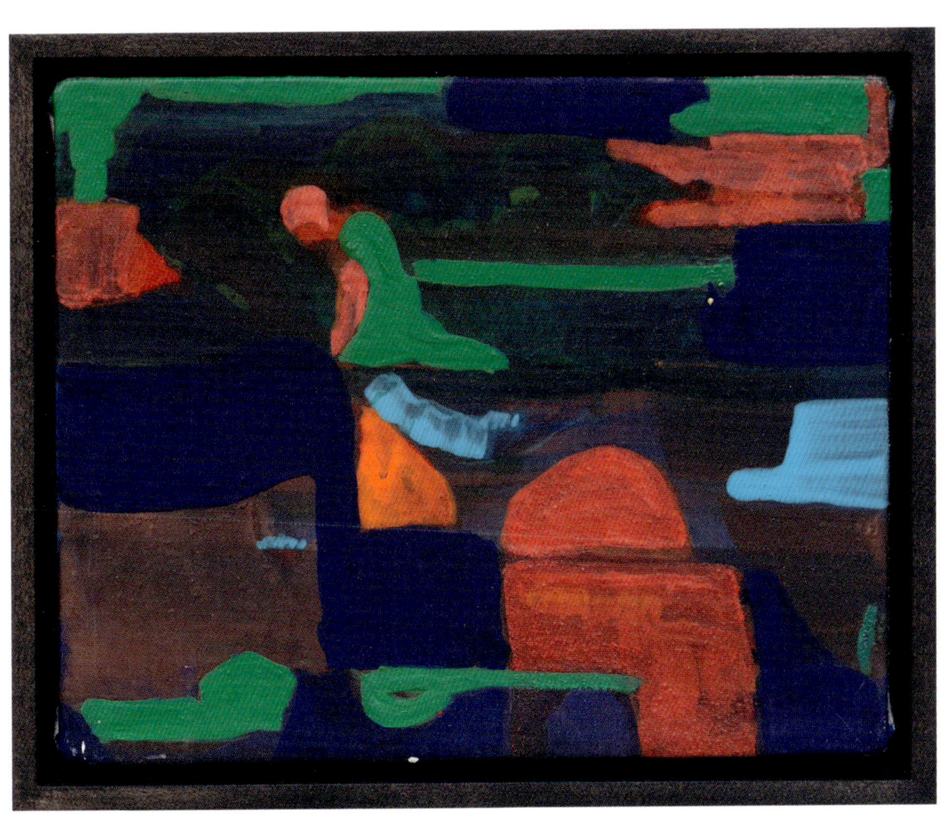

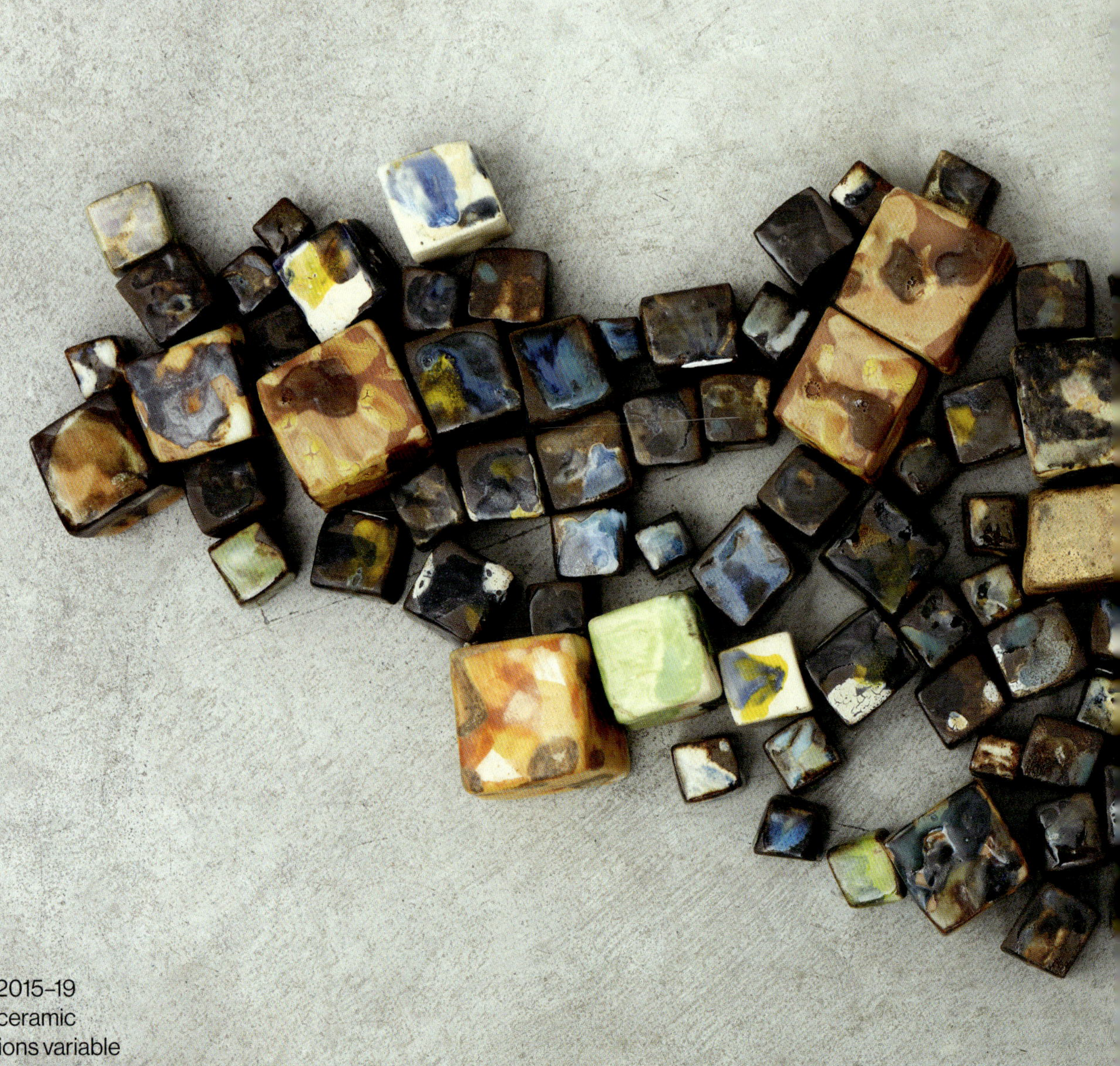

Blocks, 2015–19
Glazed ceramic
Dimensions variable

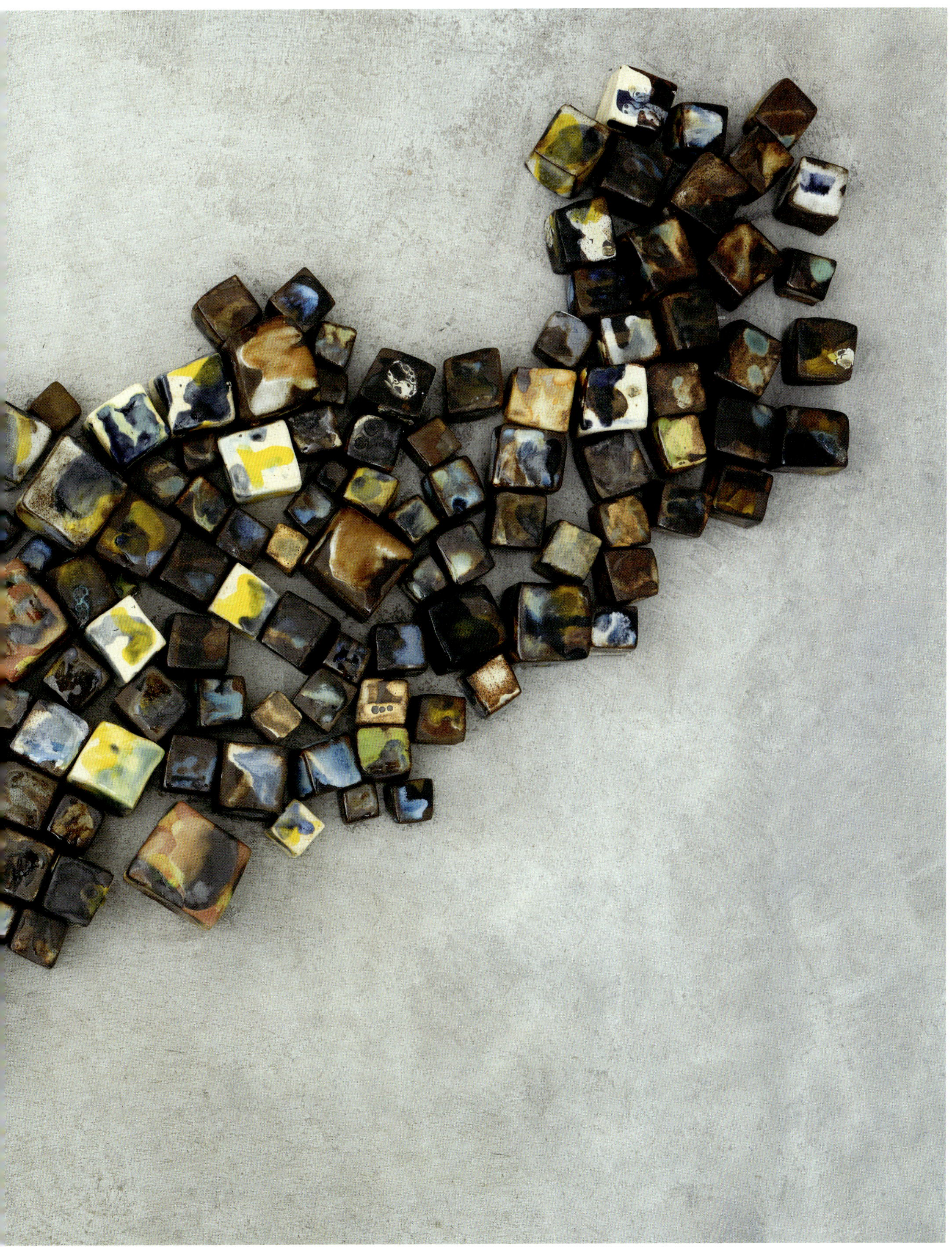

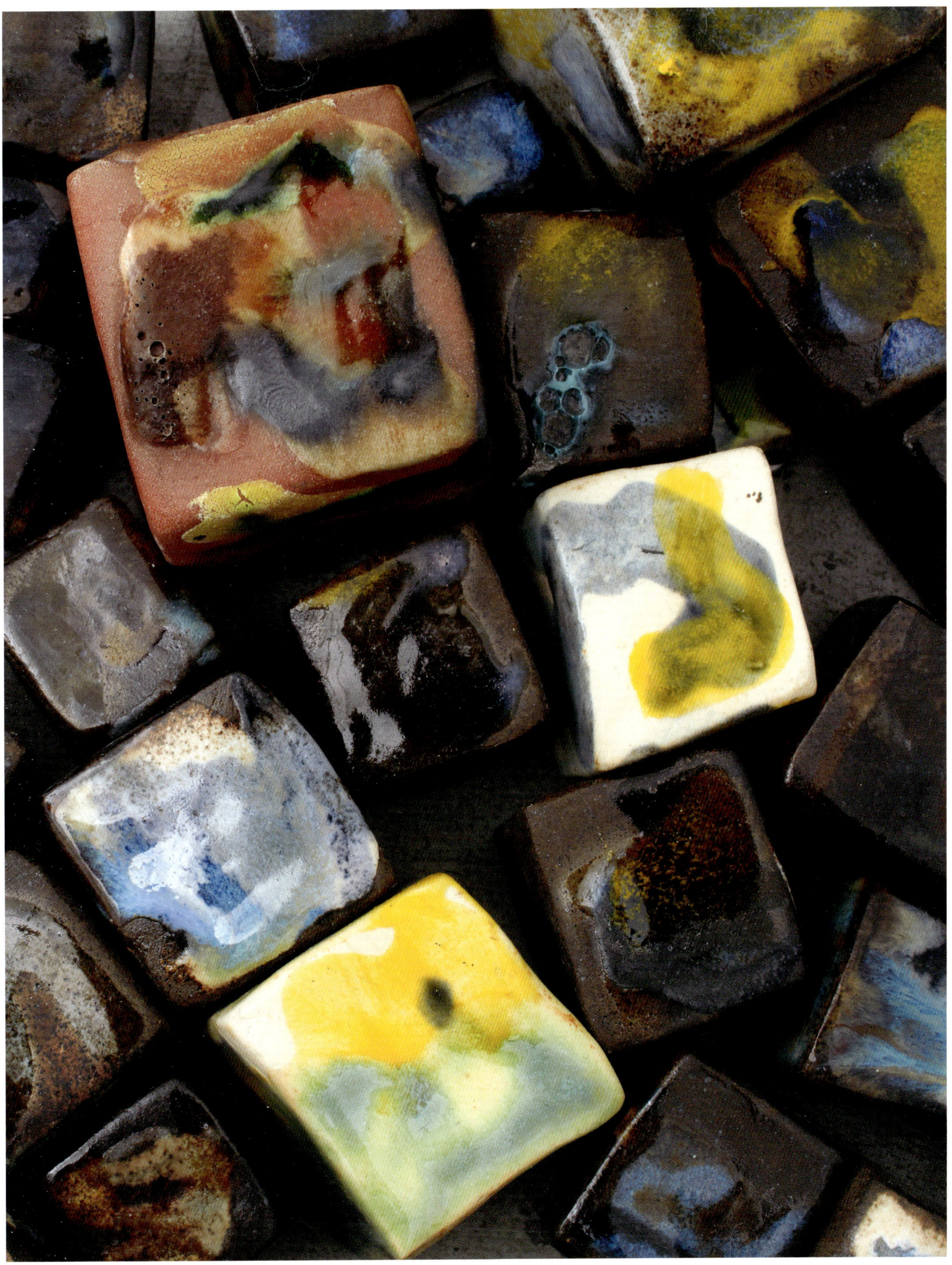

Punting Strollers, 2016
Acrylic on antique linen
18½ × 20½ inches

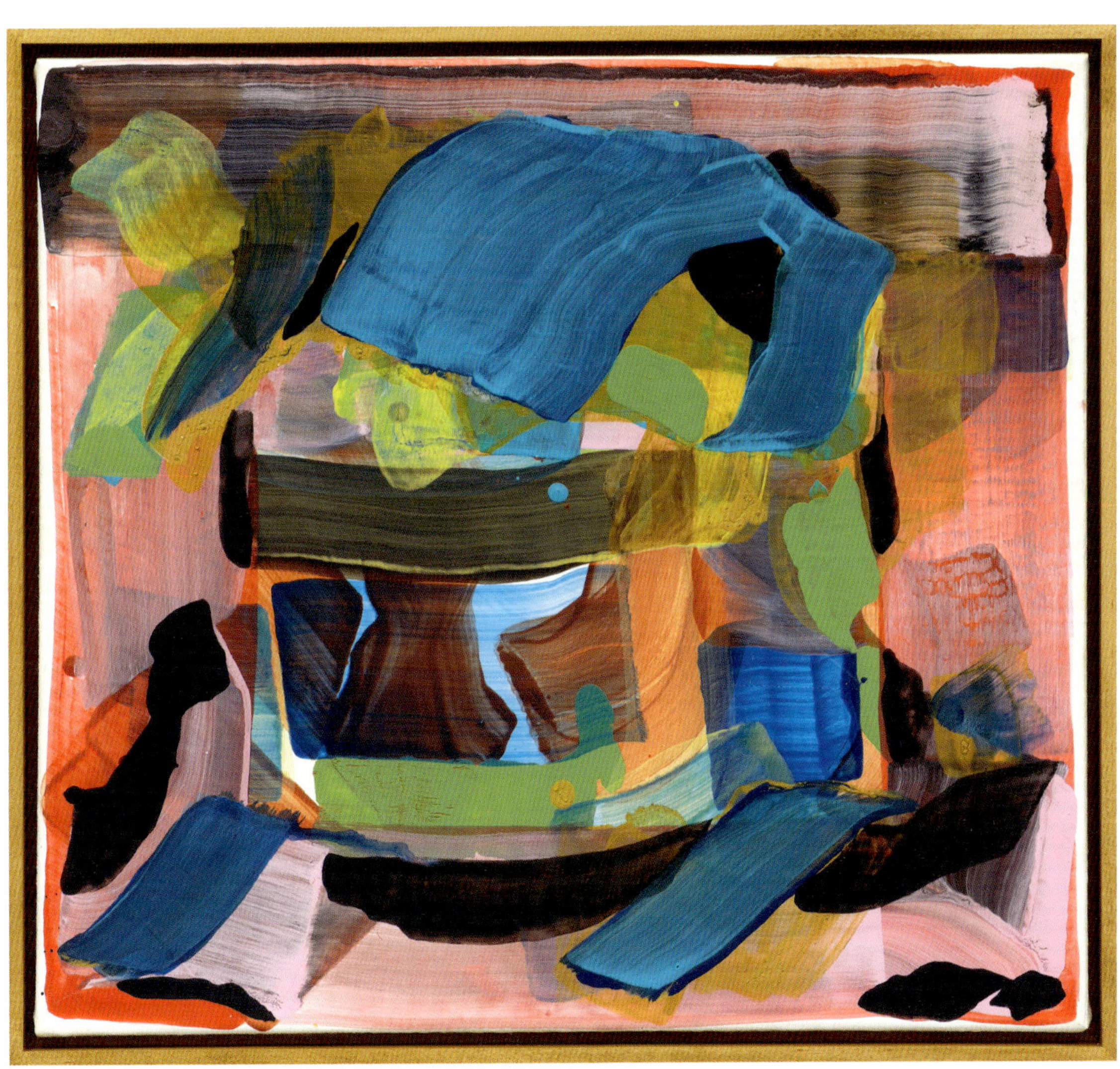

Marley Freeman
Park Closes at Midnight

Published on the occasion
of the exhibition at

Karma
188 East 2nd Street
New York, NY 10009

May 17–June 23, 2019

Edition of 750
Special edition of 50

Publication © 2019
Marley Freeman
and Karma, New York

Artwork © Marley Freeman

Of Equals © 2019
Lauren O'Neill-Butler

ISBN: 978-1-949172-26-3

Marley Freeman would like to thank:

Family and friends
Janice Guy
Brendan Dugan
Siniša Mačković
Leidy Churchman
Math Bass
Sam Parker
Lander Burton
Anselm Berrigan
Karma
Parker Gallery